There's a Hole in Your Sky

Limericks you can tell to anyone

There's a Hole
in Your Sky

Limericks you can tell to anyone

Bob Scher

By Bob Scher
Drawings by Peter Szasz

Browser Books Publishing

Browser Books Publishing
2195 Fillmore Street
San Francisco, CA 94115
www.browserbooksonline.com

ISBN: 0-9772212-4-5
ISBN: 978-0-9772212-4-0
Library of Congress Control Number: 2006929585

Cover design by Mellissa Lau

To Tom O' Bedlam
May he truly rest in peace

Acknowledgments

The author gratefully acknowledges these publications in which some of these limes have previously appeared: *Material for Thought, Works and Conversations, The American Mathematical Monthly.*

Contents

Preface

It is significant that almost no limericks since Lear's have been both printable and funny enough to seem worth quoting.

George Orwell, 1945

Non-bawdy or "clean" limericks, which we call limes, predate the bawdy ones. The earliest complete example we know of is by St. Thomas Aquinas (!) (1224-1274) in *The Roman Catholic Breviary*. Some of the first known limes in English in the almost complete five-line form – i.e., without the first line rhyming – are probably those in the mad songs of wandering beggars in the 1600's, such as the well-known "Tom O'Bedlam":

> …I know more than Apollo,
> For oft when he lies sleeping
>> I see the stars
>> At mortal wars
> In the wounded welkin weeping…

Shakespeare included nearly perfect limes in Othello (Act II, Scene 3), Hamlet (Act IV, Scene 5), and King Lear (Act II, Scene 4). Robert Herrick wrote verses employing only complete limes (as in the poem "The Night Piece, To Julia"), as did W. S. Gilbert (as in the song "When a Wooer Goes A-wooing" from *Yeoman of the Guard*).

However, a lime capable of standing alone usually requires a twist or a neat turn in the last line. This is true for none of the above (except for some in "Tom O'Bedlam"), nor was it necessary since these were either written for inclusion in longer works, or else the work consisted of a sequence of limes. They are limes in form but not in essence.

In spite of the enormous number of bawdy limericks circulating in the 19th century – some obviously brilliant – the popularization of this form came with the publication of Edward Lear's *A Book of Nonsense* (1846), a collection of clean limericks whose last line usually didn't rhyme but was, instead, a repeated word. This would normally result in dull verse; however, their subtle charm was greatly enhanced by Lear's singularly whimsical drawings.

Some of our limes are not exactly "funny," but we trust they will still satisfy Orwell's intended criterion. And the incisively witty and expressive drawings of Peter Szasz do more than just illustrate the limes, they extend them into new domains.

We would also be pleased if the reader is reminded that sometimes a lime can also be genuine poetry.

YOUR SPACE IS CURVED

An impressive event, the Big Bang,
The adventure from which we all sprang;
    For some it's a passion,
    For some it's the fashion,
And others just don't give a hang.

There once was a robber named Time,
Who masked his profession in rhyme;
 He stole through the day
 And took it away,
But no one accused him of crime.

They say that space ends in a curve,
And whatever goes straight there will swerve;
    It's mainly a menace
    To those who play tennis,
Since no one can hit back a serve.

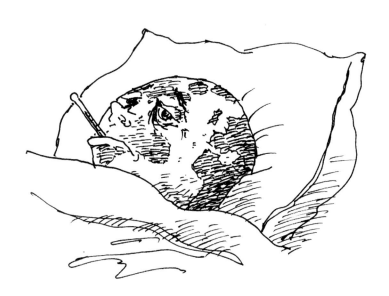

The Earth is alive, just like you
With quadrillions of things on its queue;
    Ecologically great
    In its natural state,
It can speedily bid us adieu.

An atom of heavenly blue,
In rushing to get somewhere new,
    Forgot to close up,
    So if someone goes up,
There'll be a small hole to look through.

Of Newton, they said it was his;
Then Einstein became the world's whiz,
  With deep explanation
  Of all gravitation –
But we do not know yet what it is.

Behold the Murphy of Law:
Such resistance in all that he saw!
    But to be unaware
    Or pretend it's not there
Was to him an infallible flaw.

If you fall in a hole that is black
And is totally filled up with lack,
    You'll be in defiance
    Of all of our science
If ever you find your way back.

A butterfly named Clementina
Was gliding through North Carolina;
   The move of her wing
   Isn't much of a thing,
But it changes the weather in China.

People may turn to genetics
To better their looks or athletics;
   Imagine a world
   Where muscles unfurled,
And nobody needed cosmetics.

A microscope focused with care
May even show things that aren't there,
    But negative matter
    Would cause it to shatter
And give me a positive scare.

For people to get to the stars,
They will have to reckon with Mars.
    On Mars you will never
    Find Martians. They're clever.
However, you'll find them in bars.

A computer was starting to think
That the world was approaching the brink:
   "I know my acumen
   Is better than human,
But all I want now is a drink."

There is nuclear fission and fusion,
Whose division breeds active intrusion;
   While fusion is mild,
   Some fission is wild
And comes to a violent conclusion.

A woman who lived in a book
Came out one day for a look;
   She dined upon sedge
   And fished off the edge
Of a beautiful, silvery brook.

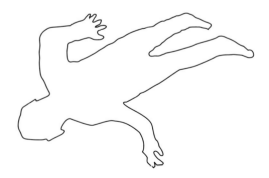

PEOPLE AND OTHERS IN TROUBLE

A shadow at noon in the park
Made a brilliant, insightful remark:
    "I know that this light
     Is unbearably bright,
But wherever I am it's still dark."

While making a mirror inspection,
Dracula saw his reflection!
    It's a volume of woe
    For a vampire to know
That he has an unpleasant complexion.

There once was a man who was certain
The world was a stage with a curtain;
    He played his last role
    And when placed in a hole
He said, "Please would you drop some dessert in."

A woman bought camels on sale
And received thirty mammals by rail;
    "It's much cheaper, by far,"
    Said a man in a bar,
"If you have them all shipped through the mail."

꙰

An executive using his cell
Dialed long distance to hell;
    He asked of the devil
     "Be gracious, and level."
The devil replied, "All is well."

A man in a pink and blue bubble
Stretched himself till he was double;
　　And just for some pranks,
　　They floated through banks,
And got into serious trouble.

A girl who went up in a kite
Went up in the air out of sight.
   She finally came down
   On the outside of town
And said that the ride was just right.

From his prison of ice they defrosted him,
Then hordes of reporters accosted him;
    A ten-thousand-year old
    Is terribly cold,
And their well-meaning efforts exhausted him.

A completely incompetent wizard
Mistakenly summoned a blizzard;
   When harshly accused
   He got quite confused
And turned himself into a lizard.

A man with an oversized leg
Got stuck in an oversized keg.
   When breakfast came round
   On his plate the man found
A preposterous oversized egg.

A man with a powerful itch
To be handsome and crooked and rich
   Had plans far and wide,
   Except one day, he died –
For him an unfortunate hitch.

A contradictory sleuth
Who thought he was old in his youth,
    Pursued the absurd,
    Which often occurred,
And negated his notion of truth.

There was a magician quite fond
Of waving his magical wand.
    One day when he waved
    The wand misbehaved
And emailed him to The Beyond.

The man in the moon made a moan –
He was pining from shining alone –
    Then discovered a bride
    On his opposite side
And called her up on the phone.

To be selling saltpeter excluded him
From places where folks had saluted him,
    Without – it's a fact –
    The slightest of tact;
Wherever he went they just booted him.

ANIMAL PASSIONS

A mouse is better than mice—
A populous pantry's not nice
   For a blend of minuteness,
   Astuteness, and cuteness,
A single one

                will suffice.

A mouse is better than mice;
A populous pantry's not nice;
    For a blend of minuteness,
    Astuteness, and cuteness,
A single one will suffice.

There was once a confused kangaroo
Who for some reason only said "Moo!"
　　When confronted by cows
　　With implacable brows,
It hopped in the air and it flew.

A Tyrannosaurus Rex
Was pursuing the opposite sex;
    But then Nature blinked,
    Which made them extinct.
This is not what a creature expects.

LIZARD IN REPOSE

A lizard who slept on a stone
Was placed in a gallery and shown.
   Its manner was noble,
   Its body, immobile,
But what it was thinking's unknown.

A boppity bounding bat
Went floppity down on my hat.
    I ran through the night
    In a desperate flight,
But it only desired a chat.

There once was a talented cheetah
Who was perfect at singing Aida;
    But because at close range
     She looked totally strange,
She would only appear *incognita*.

An otter at home in the water
Said, "Look at my beautiful daughter –
　　She walks on the sand
　　And plays in a band,
But these aren't the things that I taught her!"

If a porcupine's turning her back on you,
She's not planning to make an attack on you;
    But if you provoke her,
    Disturb her, or poke her,
A lot of her quills will land smack on you.

An ostrich as quick as a flash
Beat them all in the hundred-yard dash.
   But to earn a good wage
   It cavorted on stage,
A preposterous ostrich – a smash!

A fiscally elegant auk
Decided to learn how to talk;
    It uttered in syllables
    All of its billables,
Causing its debtors to squawk.

A remarkably civilized squirrel
Rejected most everything rural;
    He attracted a spouse
    By dancing to Strauss,
And that singular squirrel became plural.

He powered the golf ball so high,
It came down on a grandmother's pie.
    But she was ecstatic,
    A golfing fanatic,
And drove the ball back to the guy.

"Come into my parlor," said Spider;
Fly entered and sat down beside her;
 Then he issued a spell
 Under which Spider fell
Because Fly's cosmic vision was wider.

A goat who needed a shave
Was floating on top of a wave;
    They cried out, "How silly!"
    "Un-goatlike!" "Un-billy!"
And no one could make him behave.

An aquavor went for a swim –
He does many strange things on a whim.
   Do not let him fret,
   Don't get him upset,
And do not go swimming with him.

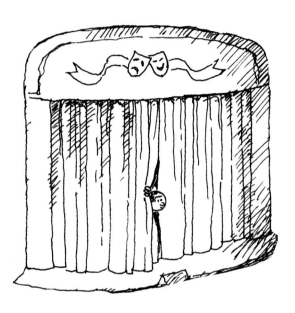

OURSELVES

There may come a memorable day
When we realize our lives are a play,
When we know in our hearts
That we must play our parts,
'Cause this theater's not going away.

What is "now?" It is never obtrusive;
All our explanations, effusive;
   Though less than a minute,
   Yet everything's in it,
But some find it strangely elusive.

And now for a serious lime,
For one that soars beyond time:
   To just comprehend,
   Let alone to transcend,
I suggest we begin with Who I'm.

The unlimited world that I see
Contains diamonds and dreams – and debris.
  So how to begin
  To take it all in
And remember that part of it's me.

GRANT PROPOSAL

You're in another dimension,
So I hope this gets Your Attention.
　Even though where You Are
　There's no time, near, or far,
I desperately need an extension.

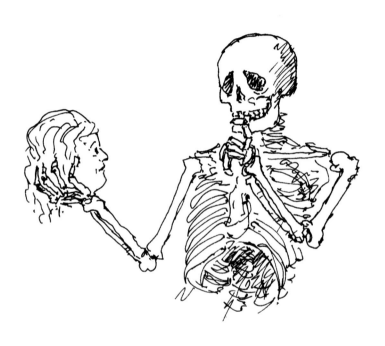

Hamlet was very confused
His Weltanshauung radically bruised;
    In the vengeance he sought
    He himself became caught,
And for some reason we're all amused.

When opinions like onions are peeled,
Often another's revealed;
    And beneath that belief
    There is often a Chief,
But our lips about this one are sealed.

When walking in weather that blistery,
Yesterday's sun is just history.
   Why sometimes the present
   Can seem so unpleasant
Remains a remarkable mystery.

Prodigious divisions of fractions –
Though better than horrid subtractions –
   For you, if you fidget
   When facing a digit,
They're not one of life's main attractions.

It pays to possess common sense
And to penetrate things that are dense;
   A good use of the brain
   Is to make matters plain,
Yet what we don't know is immense.

Are there not, among powers that be,
Wise beings that no one can see?
   For things keep on going,
   And flowing and growing;
It seems overwhelming to me.

We walk around in a stupor,
And just while we're thinking we're super,
    In the world of our acts,
    Here are the facts:
We just made our one-millionth blooper.

Most of the time you will find us
Putting self-knowledge behind us.
   As we go to and fro
   It's what we don't know:
These are the powers that bind us.

We're not just on the Earth, so let's face it:
Wherever we are, let's embrace it.
   With the Stars all around
   In the Cosmos we're bound
And we cannot remove or replace it.

Life comes to us through the senses
And penetrates all our defenses.
   There's no standard fee –
   The best things seem free –
But O, those other expenses!

To Peter, My Collaborator

With monsters I'm quite well acquainted;
They were always too scared to be painted:
    They would come in and sit
    By my door in a fit,
And whenever I *drew* them they fainted.